Running, Jumping, and Throwing— If You Can

30345000517428

Words by
Gary Paulsen

Pictures by
Heinz Kluetmeier

🄿 Childrens Press

Copyright © 1978, Raintree Publishers Limited

All rights reserved. No part of this book may be reproduced or utilized in any form or by any means, electronic or mechanical, including photocopying, recording, or by any information storage and retrieval system, without permission in writing from the Publisher. Inquiries should be addressed to Raintree Publishers Limited, 205 West Highland Avenue, Milwaukee, Wisconsin 53203.

Library of Congress Number: 77-27479

1 2 3 4 5 6 7 8 9 0 82 81 80 79 78

Printed in the United States of America.

Library of Congress Cataloging in Publication Data

Paulsen, Gary.
   Running, jumping, and throwing — if you can.

   SUMMARY: Photographs provide a humorous commentary on various aspects of professional track and field events.
   1. Track-athletics — Juvenile literature.
[1. Track and field] I. Kluetmeier, Heinz.
II. Title.
GV1060.5.P33 796.4'2 77-27479
ISBN 0-8172-1160-8 lib. bdg.

TRACK

Track is the oldest athletic event in the world.

It dates back thousands of years.

What makes it a little strange is that it's all about running and jumping and throwing things.

Which you can do any time you clean your room.

SPRINTS

Short distance *fast* running — called sprinting — is probably the quickest part of track.

The only problem is that it makes you look fuzzy and blurry.

Actually sprinting is pretty simple.
You just get a good start.

Then get as fuzzy and blurry as possible.

The person who gets the blurriest is the winner.

Another good approach to sprinting is to get a grimace on your face.

Then just move forward as fast as you can.

If you move forward fast enough you'll get all blurry and win.

Starting is the most important part
of sprinting.

The legs have to be right, hands just so,
the head down.

Just make sure you don't go to sleep.

LONG DISTANCE

Long distance running is the oldest kind of track. And it's getting more popular all the time.

The idea is pretty simple.

You just run a long way, make a face like you're going to throw up, and fall down.

The end of a long distance run is a good time to take off your shoes and put a bag of cool water on your head.

Although it seems like a lot of work just to get a cool head and sweaty feet.

Relay running is the same as long distance running except for one thing.

Right before the runner falls down, he hands a little stick to the next runner.

HURDLES

For some races the officials put little wooden highway barricades in front of the runners.

These are called hurdles.

Running the hurdles is about like all the other running. Except that the hurdles make it easier to fall down.

Running and jumping the hurdles has been called the most graceful form of track.

It's also a good way to see if your shoelaces are tied or if your socks match in color.

FIELD EVENTS

Field events are where everybody jumps or throws things. Some performers do both.

Some athletes say that their form is the most important part of winning field events.

Form is especially vital when high jumping. A small area of an arm or leg can ruin it all.

It's no wonder some jumpers wind up hating parts of their bodies.

Field events are also when broad jumpers perform.

The idea is simple. They just run as hard as they can and then jump as far as they can.

They don't get extra points for messing up the sand.

Despite what some people say, throwing the discus and the shot aren't just ways to make faces.

And it isn't called throwing the shot, either.

It's called *putting* the shot.

You're supposed to put it as far away as possible.

It is also during the field events that people throw their spears.

The spears are called javelins.

It's a good idea not to get a javelin thrower mad at you.

Some throwers get so worried about how they look that they try to watch themselves throwing.

Which, of course, could lead to a sprained neck.

The main thing to remember about track is to remove your shoes immediately after an event.

Your poor aching feet will need a break.